D0292145

# Violent
## Weather
### Thunderstorms, Tornadoes, and Hurricanes

By Andrew Collins

NATIONAL GEOGRAPHIC

Washington D.C.

One of the world's largest nonprofit scientific and educational organizations, the National Geographic Society was founded in 1888 "for the increase and diffusion of geographic knowledge." Fulfilling this mission, the Society educates and inspires millions every day through its magazines, books, television programs, videos, maps and atlases, research grants, the National Geographic Bee, teacher workshops, and innovative classroom materials. The Society is supported through membership dues, charitable gifts, and income from the sale of its educational products. This support is vital to National Geographic's mission to increase global understanding and promote conservation of our planet through exploration, research, and education.

For more information, please call
1-800-NGS-LINE (647-5463) or write to the following address:
National Geographic Society
1145 17th Street N.W.
Washington, D.C. 20036-4688
U.S.A.

For information about special discounts for bulk purchases, please contact
National Geographic Books Special Sales at ngspecsales@ngs.org

Visit the Society's Web site: www.nationalgeographic.com

**Library of Congress Cataloging-in-Publication Data**

Collins, Andrew.
  Violent weather : thunderstorms, tornadoes, and hurricanes / by Andrew Collins.
    p. cm. -- (National Geographic science chapters)
  Includes index.
  ISBN-13: 978-0-7922-5947-3 (library binding)
  ISBN-10: 0-7922-5947-5 (library binding)
  1. Thunderstorms. 2. Tornadoes. 3. Hurricanes. I. Title. II. Series.
  QC968.C65 2006
  551.55--dc22

                                        2006016338

**Photo Credits**
Front Cover: © Burton Mcneely/ Getty Images; Spine: © Todd Gipstein/ National Geographic Image Collection; Endpaper: © Todd Gipstein/ National Geographic Image Collection; 0-1: © Carsten Peter/ National Geographic Image Collection; 4: © Photolibrary.com; 5: © PhotoDisc/ Getty Images; 6: © Bruce A. Dale/ National Geographic Image Collection; 8: © Medford Taylor/ National Geographic Image Collection; 12: © Getty Images; 14: © Richard Olsenius/ National Geographic Image Collection; 16: © Sarah Leen/ National Geographic Image Collection; 18: © Getty Images; 19: © Carsten Peter/ National Geographic/ Getty Images; 20-21: © Getty Images; 22: © Carsten Peter/ National Geographic Image Collection; 24: © Joe Raedle/ Reportage/ Getty Images; 26: © Photolibrary.com; 28: © Chris Graythen/ Getty Images; 29: © Getty Images; 30-31: © Photolibrary.com; 32 (top): © Jim Reed/ Corbis; 32 (bottom): © PhotoDisc/ Getty Images; 34: © Photolibrary.com; 35: © Raul Touzon/ National Geographic/ Getty Images; Illustrations by Dimitrios Prokopis.

# Contents

Dark storm clouds often
mean violent weather
is approaching.

# Violent Weather

**A**ir is all around us. We can't see it, but we can feel it when it blows. When the wind blows, air from somewhere else moves in. The new air might be warmer or cooler, drier or wetter. When two bodies of air collide, or crash into each other, storms develop. Storms are periods of violent weather.

The swirling winds of a tornado are one kind of violent weather.

Powerful lightning bolts shoot from the sky during a thunderstorm.

# Chapter 1

# Thunderstorms

It's a warm summer day. Late in the afternoon, clouds roll in and the sky turns dark. The wind starts to blow. The temperature drops. A bright light flashes across the sky. A thundering crash booms in the distance. Soon rain will pour from the sky. A thunderstorm is approaching.

Thunderstorms are storms that produce lightning and thunder. They often cause heavy rain and strong winds. Thunderstorms are the most common of all severe, or violent, storms. Luckily, thunderstorms don't usually last a long time. Most are over within an hour or two.

## Why Thunderstorms Form

Thunderstorms form when a body of cold air high in the sky crashes into warm, moist air that is low to the ground. The warm air moves upward, and the two types of air mix. Huge, dark, anvil-shaped clouds form. They bring lightning, thunder, and heavy rain. Most thunderstorms occur in the spring and summer months.

Most thunderstorms happen in the afternoon or evening.

# How Thunderstorms Form

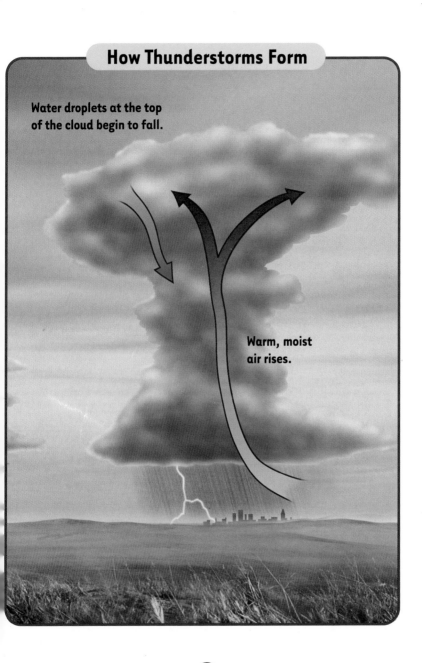

Water droplets at the top of the cloud begin to fall.

Warm, moist air rises.

## Thunder and Lightning

Thunder is loud, but it can't hurt you. Lightning can. A lightning bolt is a giant spark of electricity. As the air mixes within a storm cloud, electricity builds up. When enough electricity builds up, a giant spark of lightning results.

When lightning flashes, a great amount of heat is released. The heat warms the air, causing it to expand with an explosion. The expanding air creates the thunder we hear.

Light travels faster than sound. As a result, we typically see lightning before we hear the accompanying thunder.

At any given point in time, 1,800 thunderstorms are happening somewhere on Earth.

## Thunderstorm Damage

Thunderstorms can be dangerous. Strong winds can knock down trees and power lines. Heavy rains can cause flooding. Every year lightning kills about 100 people in the United States.

## Staying Safe

You can stay safe during a thunderstorm if you follow these safety tips.

*If you are inside*

- Stay indoors.
- Don't use the telephone or electrical equipment such as a computer or a television because lightning can strike the electrical wires that connect to your house and give you a shock.
- Stay out of the bathtub or shower because water conducts electricity.

*If you are outside*

- Seek shelter.
- Get out of the water and small boats.
- If you can't go inside, find a low spot away from trees or poles. Squat down and cover your head. Don't lie on the ground.

◀ The huge amount of rain dropped during a thunderstorm can cause flash flooding.

Tornadoes are sometimes called twisters because of their strong, spinning winds.

# Chapter 2

# Tornadoes

Severe thunderstorms have replaced the calm of a sunny summer afternoon. As the thunderstorms pass through, the wind grows stronger and stronger. The sound of the wind becomes so loud it is almost deafening. It sounds as though several jet airplanes are taking off at once. Dirt flies through the air. A tornado is coming.

A tornado is a funnel-shaped column of strong wind that stretches from a storm cloud to the ground. Tornadoes are the most violent of all storms. The winds in the strongest tornadoes can spin at more than 300 miles (480 km) per hour.

## Why Tornadoes Form

Tornadoes form when the cool air of a storm cloud settles on top of warm air and traps it. When some of the warm air breaks through the cool air, it spirals, or spins, upward. This creates the swirling wind of a funnel cloud.

Weak tornadoes often look like long, thin ropes.

# How Tornadoes Form

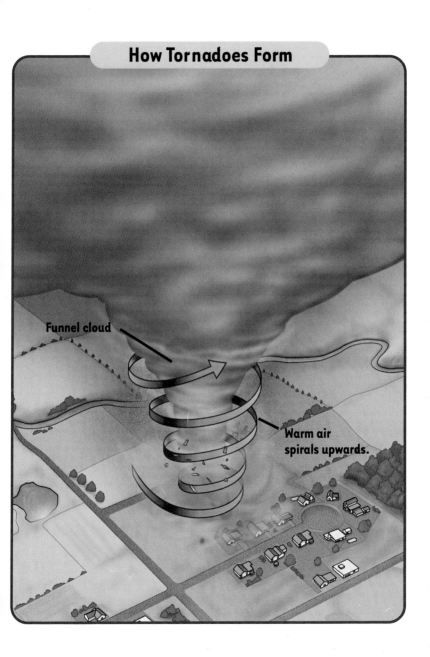

Funnel cloud

Warm air spirals upwards.

A tornado's winds are strong enough to imbed a coat hanger and a bracket in a tree.

## Tornado Damage

A tornado's funnel cloud acts like a giant vacuum cleaner. When it touches the ground, it picks up everything in its path—trees, cars, even the roofs off houses. A funnel cloud looks dark because of all the dirt and trash flying around in the spinning wind.

◀ A tornado's strong winds will destroy everything in its path.

Most tornadoes last less than 15 minutes, but they can be deadly. A powerful twister can tear a house apart and throw the pieces in all directions. Every year tornadoes in the United States kill about 100 people and cause millions of dollars worth of damage.

Tornadoes are most likely to occur in places shown in orange.

A tornado can cause this kind of damage in less than a minute.

Tornadoes can occur anywhere in the world, but more tornadoes form in the United States than in any other country. The central part of the country—from north Texas to Iowa—is known as Tornado Alley. Hundreds of tornadoes occur here each year.

Storm chasers are people who gather data about tornadoes. These storm chasers have stopped to drop a weather probe in this tornado's path.

## Staying Safe

The national weather service warns us when there are severe storms. The best way to stay safe is to pay attention to these warnings.

A *tornado watch* means weather conditions are right for a tornado to form. Stay alert to warnings and be prepared to take shelter.

A *tornado warning* means a tornado has been seen in the area. If you hear a tornado warning, take shelter.

- Go to the basement or lowest level of your house. Crouch under the stairs or heavy furniture. Cover your head.
- If you can't go inside, lie down in a ditch or other low area. Get out of cars.

# Chapter 3

# Hurricanes

Howling winds bend the trees nearly to the ground. Heavy rain pours from the sky. People have boarded up their windows. They are heading inland until the storm passes. A massive hurricane is heading towards shore.

A hurricane is a huge, swirling storm that forms over warm ocean waters. Hurricanes are the largest and most destructive of all storms. They can measure 500 miles (800 km) across and can cause high winds and heavy rain as far as 250 miles (400 km) away.

The strong winds of an approaching hurricane make it difficult to walk on the beach.

## Why Hurricanes Form

Hurricanes form when a group of thunderstorms come together over a warm sea to form a large storm. The storm clouds spin together in a circle. The sea provides the storm with energy and moisture. It becomes bigger and stronger. At the center of the storm is a calm area called the "eye."

This picture of a hurricane was taken from space.

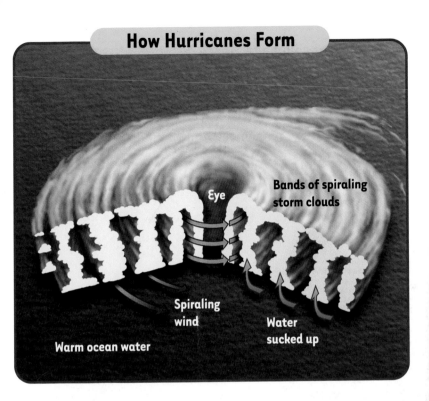

## How Hurricanes Form

Bands of spiraling storm clouds

Eye

Spiraling wind

Water sucked up

Warm ocean water

The clouds spin around the eye very quickly. When the winds in the spinning storm reach 74 miles (119 km) per hour, the storm is called a hurricane.

As the hurricane moves across the ocean, a wall of seawater called a storm surge forms under the storm. This huge wave can cause a lot of damage when it hits the coast.

## Hurricane Damage

When hurricanes move over land, they destroy things in their path. As scary as the winds are, most hurricane damage is caused by flooding from heavy rains and huge waves. Roads, houses, and cars can be swept away. In 1991 a hurricane killed 135,000 people in Asia. A hurricane flooded the city of New Orleans in 2005.

Hurricane Katrina flooded the streets of New Orleans.

A storm surge floods coastal areas.

After a major hurricane blows through, people need to clean up the rubble that's left behind.

Hurricanes are called different things in different parts of the world. These storms are called typhoons when they form in the western Pacific Ocean. They are called cyclones in Australia and countries around the Indian Ocean.

Hurricanes form in the parts of the ocean shown in yellow. Arrows show the direction they travel.

▲ People prepare for a hurricane by boarding up windows.

◀ Coastal communities know ahead of time how they'll evacuate if a hurricane comes their way.

## Staying Safe

The weather service tracks hurricanes and predicts when and where they will come ashore. They warn people when it's not safe to stay along the coast. The best way to stay safe is to follow these warnings.

A *hurricane watch* means a hurricane is possible within 36 hours. Stay alert to warnings and gather items for a disaster supply kit:
- Food and water for two weeks
- Flashlight and batteries
- Change of clothing and blankets
- Portable radio
- First aid kit

A *hurricane warning* means a hurricane is expected within 24 hours. You may be asked to evacuate, or leave your home. If you're not asked to evacuate, stay inside until the storm has passed.

Meteorologists use weather balloons to gather data about the weather.

# Chapter 4

# Weather Watch

**P**redicting and tracking storms is a big job. Meteorologists are scientists who study the weather. They use satellites, weather balloons, and other tools to gather information about changing weather conditions. They use this information to make predictions about when and where storms will form. Their predictions can help keep people safe from dangerous storms.

A meteorologist shows a hurricane's path on the local weather forecast.

# How to Write an A+ Report

## 1. Choose a topic.

- Find something that interests you.
- Make sure it is not too big or too small.

## 2. Find sources.

- Ask your librarian for help.
- Use many different sources: books, magazine articles, and websites.

## 3. Gather information.

- Take notes. Write down the big ideas and interesting details.
- Use your own words.

## 4. Organize information.

- Sort your notes into groups that make sense.

- Make an outline. Put your groups of notes in the order you want to write your report.

## 5. Write your report.

- Write an introduction that tells what the report is about.

- Use your outline and notes as you write to make sure you say everything you want to say in the order you want to say it.

- Write an ending that tells about your report.

- Write a title.

## 6. Revise and edit your report.

- Read your report to make sure it makes sense.

- Read it again to check spelling, punctuation, and grammar.

## 7. Hand in your report!

# Glossary

| | |
|---|---|
| **electricity** | a form of energy |
| **energy** | power or strength |
| **expand** | to get bigger |
| **flooding** | the flow of water over normally dry land |
| **hurricane** | a huge, swirling storm that forms over ocean waters |
| **lightning** | a flash of light caused by a giant spark of electricity in a storm cloud |
| **meteorologist** | a person who studies the weather |
| **satellite** | a machine that orbits the Earth, recording weather conditions on Earth |
| **storm** | a period of violent weather |
| **storm surge** | a huge wave that forms beneath a hurricane |
| **thunder** | the noise heard after lightning flashes |
| **thunderstorm** | a storm that produces lightning and thunder |
| **tornado** | a funnel-shaped column of spinning wind |

# Further Reading

### • Books •

Burt, Christopher. *Extreme Weather: A Guide and Record Book*. New York, NY: W.W. Norton and Company, 2004. Grades 7-12, 304 pages.

Grace, Catherine O'Neill. *Forces of Nature: The Awesome Power of Volcanoes, Earthquakes, and Tornadoes*. Washington, DC: National Geographic Society, 2004. Ages 9-12, 64 pages.

Maslin, Mark. *Storms (Restless Planet)*. Chicago, IL Raintree, 2000. Ages 9-12, 48 pages.

Simon, Seymour. *Hurricanes*. New York, NY: Harper Trophy, 2003. Ages 9-12, 32 pages.

Simon, Seymour. *Lightning*. New York, NY: Harper Trophy, 1999. Ages 9-12, 32 pages.

Simon, Seymour. *Storms*. New York, NY: Harper Trophy, 2000. Ages 9-12, 32 pages.

Simon, Seymour. *Tornadoes*. New York, NY: Harper Trophy, 1999. Ages 9-12, 32 pages.

*Weather (First Pocket Guide Series)*. Washington, DC: National Geographic Society, 2001. Ages 8-10, 80 pages.

### • Websites •

Extreme Science
http://www.extremescience.com/weatherport.htm

Federal Emergency Management Agency
http://www.fema.gov/kids/thunder.htm
http://www.fema.gov/kids/tornado.htm
http://www.fema.gov/kids/hurr.htm

National Geographic Society: Forces of Nature
http://www.nationalgeographic.com/forcesofnature/interactive/index.html

National Oceanic and Atmospheric Administration
http://www.noaa.gov/

USA Today
http://www.usatoday.com/weather/resources/basics/thunderstorms.htm

# Index